MUSINGS OF THE AWAKENING SOUL

AN ANTHOLOGY BY
DR. PALLAVI KWATRA
IMAGES BY SAN DEEP

Invincible Publishers

First published in India in 2017 by Invincible Publishers

ISBN: 978-93-86148-71-1

Invincible Publishers
G-120, Sushant Lok III, Sector 57, Gurgaon-122002

Opposite Kasturba Ashram, Radaur Distt Yamuna Nagar, Haryana- 135133

Digitally Printed at Replika Press Pvt. Ltd.

Bhagwan Ramana
Maharishi

Dedicated to all the Teachers, Gurus and Friends who manifested as the pure self in this soul journey. May all be blessed ! Shanti Om!

Khoob sa pyaar (Loads of Love) to my Husband; Dr Sundeep Khurana, My Dad; Late Prithviraj Kwatra, My Mom; Late Adarsh Kwatra and My Daughters, Dhwani & Suhaani.

I am deeply grateful to
Dr Tina M Benson for adding a foreward to the book
Ram Das batchelder for the book back cover
San deep for the images and book cover
Kailasam Berke for unveiling this book
May god bless them….

Synopsis

In today's world of technology, where one can know about everything possible starting from quantum entanglement to doing a graffiti bun with your untamed hair, we might seem to be under a magnified illusion of "super evolution". Humanity at its peak of knowledge and progress is however thirsty for a whole lot more. Each of us need the succor of sitting beneath a fruit laden tree on a raging hot summer day, a river serenely flowing by that heartily is willing to quench our thirst, the warm embrace of mother earth, rains in which we can dance to conceal our tears, soul co travelers who assist and propel us on our journeys of self awakening, a beloved that engulfs us with a sacred love and a satiated seat of peaceful awareness in the mid chaos of our turbulent and fleeting lives.

The soul needs its nourishment in ways similar to the body and the mind. Through ages infinite, art has played a major role to quench this soul starvation. In various forms of work like paintings, photographs, sculpture, theatre, prose and poetry, art has renewed the way that we celebrate life. This book endeavors to inter mingle such forms and bring to the reader to heal himself in this construct. Here, we have tried to do a fusion of words and images which speak what remains limited by words. I am deeply grateful to San deep for his precious contributions to make a wholesome expression of my poems through his image inputs.

A spiritual awakening is nothing short of a catastrophe, a black hole in space birthing millions of constellations of light. A paradox of the highest genre, an occurrence heralding a paradigm shift in soul consciousness. A destination of peace, stillness and non identity which is reached by the spiritual traveler who is struck by perennial delusions and disappointments. A spiritual awakening is a fine distillation of consciousness to arrive at the primordial truth. Seekers are horribly confused people who resemble the snake shedding old skin, blissfully ecstatic in their new found look and yet, grieving over their amputating egos. In their ageless strife, the spiritual warrior is so used to upholding his armor in the world, needs to shun this ammunition and expose his baring soul to the scorching suns of a stilled time. In the world that he has known of till now, the knowledge of self protection in the face of strife and a struggle that goes on is the benchmark of activity. When one has been nurtured by these conditionings, it often becomes impossible to fathom surrender and the rewards of stilling all activity.

These poems spring from a deep universal intelligence, a heart of overwhelming compassion and are an intricate interplay of a spiritual seeker's psyche. In various shades, it points to his personal truth. Every artist has a signature style, so must I also be the same? But it is my heartfelt wish that I succumb to not a single modality of presentation, but let the truth flow uninhibited through my veins. This book is a narrative of such a seeker who tries to solace his aching soul by drenching its multi fold experiences in the most appropriate words possible.

Dialect is considered good communication but it offers poor translations in matters of the heart. However with my humblest efforts, with the aid of words, I seek to accompany my co travelers to alternating zones of light and darkness. As we walk these steps together, we unravel newer realizations and undisclosed dimensions. On my enchanting journey to deeper level of subconscious realms, I excavated not only treasures, but also rocks. In deep gratitude for both of these, I humbly bow to have always been led by them to the light. As a seeker, sometimes I visited colonies of sufi devotion, and on other times, the mind boggling stupor of great mystics. Sometimes, I was in a hermit's form and at others, I just lurked at the windows being a dispassionate observer. My heart sometimes panged with devotion and at other instances, I found myself in dusky caves of a detached meditating yogi. There were the intellectual interrogations of Advaita, the upheaval of Buddhist chants and sometimes the drenching in plain surrender. At one time, I was a healer who channeled the divine light, at others, a tantric practioner experimenting deeply with enlightened sexuality. Sometimes, I travelled at lightening pace and at others, each step was a peril. Here is a collection of poems which brought out the climate within me at that passing point of time. None are the same, and, yet, they all are about me. It is my prayer and wish that all co travelers en route to the light will be able to relate to these writings with a stark similarity to their own path and still uniquely give them the freedom and non inhibition to support, nurture, listen and care for others.

Truth in its pure form can touch, heal and revive aching souls. The light of the higher self did this healing to me and as I re birthed in this glorious grace, it commanded me to carry forth the legacy of this monumental and sacred work. The poems flow across ten subtitles starting from the blossoming and flowering in the ambience of the guru, moving across the expanse of opening of the heart to love that starts with the beloved, culminating in the seeker becoming love himself. Through the route of surrender, the seeker comes to rest his awareness in the eternal present, where he witnesses every occurrence without any mental or conditioned bias. He is ever grateful for whatever befalls his path, even welcoming and surviving the dark phases of deep suffering and sorrow in his life. As he goes through these phases, he inculcates dispassion that he uses as a springboard to go deeper within. His story then begins to take a new turn as all these globalize him to become a full grown human being…wise, expanded, compassionate, pure and detached. He emerges as a fragrant and well groomed tree laden with flowers and fruits, where the others of his species can come and rest at.

My vision for my friends is a world where we are unashamed to claim our weaknesses, failures and tears. In such a way, we can walk together supporting each other and helping stumbling feet to anchor soil. If I am able to play some role in this grand drama, I will consider mine as a life well lived.

In the sacred fire of this time and space, co join me in this scintillating journey to the light.

Dr Pallavi Kwatra
Author of 9 months:
An involution to evolution &
Be Love; An anthology of poems.
E mail: Pallavi_kwatra@yahoomail.com

San deep.... A signature on flowing waters

San deep.... A signature on flowing waters

Images and words... outpourings that spill from a void of unending compassion... a being which leans not on any form or the structure of time or identities... San deep (fondly called San) is aptly described in a single word.... "A BLESSING"

Encounters with him move one in spirit and invoke a karuna (compassion) and realization for one's own being. His non identity includes in it the penetrating wisdom of Advaita and Zen on one hand and on the other the surrender and befikri of sufi mystics. He is a Pandora box which always has something to lend to anyone who seeks him and at the same time.... If one were to put one's hand in the box to retrieve some magic....all one can find is a vacancy that one is pulled unto. San's marvelous and majestic life has no seeking of anything whatsoever and is a shade one finds himself in...without any exchange...it knows only of giving and offering itself, and as oblivious as the sunlight and rain that befalls on this world without discrimination.... San is a phenomenon that applies universally to all. He is neither a guru, nor a master, neither a seeker, nor a sadhak... he is neither enlightened, nor ignorant.... He JUST IS...San's following words are apt in describing who he himself is...

"Idling under a tree, chewing blades of grass....

watch a world pass by….

Once in a while, saunter to a nearby gushing brook….and sign a signature on the flowing waters….

In the stroke of the signing…..it's very erasure."

All imagery along with the cover page of this book are channeled through him. His impressions and fireworks of creativity in forms of imagery, videos and written word can be reached out by visiting his facebook page…THE PLAY OF PIXELS.

I am, but a single mote of sand ….that was lucky enough to get carried away by his drizzle …..in that single point of contact, the dissolution overtook my being….

In reverence and love…..
Pallavi.

Foreward

In the spiritual pantheon of Hinduism, the number 108 holds a particularly potent meaning...there are 108 Puranas, 108 Upanishads, 108 gopis in Vrindavan, 108 beads of a meditation mala, as well as 54 letters in Sanskrit – each of which can be considered both masculine (Shiva) and feminine (Shakti), totaling 108.

Using this number as her guide, poet and author Pallavi Kwatra's new book is an extraordinary beacon of light for all those on, or aspiring to be on, a spiritual path. From the laying of one's burdens at the feet of the Guru, through the agonizing dissolution of identification with one's ego self, the surrender and transformation of one's sorrows and desires, to the illumination of one's own most brilliant divine nature, Kwatra guides the reader by the hand through her poems as if to say, "Come...walk with me...here is the way."Using words imbued with the very illumination of which she speaks, Kwatra says:

"The descent of the mind from royal chariots
Into the humble abode of my heart.
A soundless journey that explodes with the light
This pious merger is both the means and the end As the
"I" in me has encountered It's
Righteous consummation"

Each poem in this magnificent compilation is as if a stone on the darkened path, helping to guide the reader's way in the dark. From the devastating disillusionments to the ecstatic heights of both personal and divine love,

Kwatra reminds us:

"The murmur is most often of love
When words are sparingly used.
Awaken, bow and surrender
To the mightiness of love.
Nothing else is more worthy
Of your divine prostration."

Rivaling the greatest devotional poetry of Rilke, Rumi, Mirabai, and Hafiz, Kwatra's devotion to love cries out:

"I and you
In the lap of a beautiful dream.
I sing for you..you dance for me.
The left over wine in the cups
drooling with the ecstasy
of our lips upon them.
We can neither sleep, nor lie awake.
Inebriated with a divine hangover.
Lust has now given up on us,
Only love rides high.
Intoxicated fervor,
And the nakedness of truth.
No distances separate the bodies and mind...
You are all raw
And I have lost my shame.
We exchange turns
To peak to holy orgasms..
The infinities lie aghast
At such a careless spill ...
Pray...Who will lead us home
From this ***misplaced tavern****."*

And yet, embedded in the notion of *"this misplaced tavern,"* is the awareness every spiritual aspirant eventually arrives at...the lover one has sought resides within. The greatest love of all is waiting for the one who has the temerity to surrender all outward seeking and make the arduous turn inward.

Kwatra is the penultimate spiritual guide in this most lovely and rewarding collection. Her poems will illuminate, shatter, beckon, accompany, inspire, guide, and awaken you on your journey. As in the poem below, let her gift you her "oars" so you too may celebrate!

"On the voyage of truth ,
I set forth, my sail a mast.
You gift me oars,
And terminate all safe harbor.
The world fades at the faraway horizon,
The dusk of dispassion colors my sky,
In the infinite oblivion,
I still to all pace.
The stars are above me,
The ocean below.
In this affirming absence,
All of me loses form.
My ego stands widowed from me,
And in this abandonment,I celebrate!"

And become as she says, ***"a wanderer... transmuted into the cosmic mind."***

Tina M. Benson, M.A.

Author of, "*A Woman Unto Herself: A Different Kind of Love Story*", and "*Soul whisperings: Erotic and Devotional Love Poems for an Outer or Inner Beloved.*"

REFLECTIONS

It is an honor to partake in this celebration of life where voice is given to the seemingly infinite range of emotions that thread us all in shared humanity, yet align us with something much greater—something hidden in plain sight yet as strong as gravity itself. No matter what our lineage of teachers or ancestry, Pallavi speaks from her heart, giving voice, depth and character to the universal language of love, devotion and longing which dissolves the boundaries of time, space and race understood by all.

To me, these poems are like prayer lamps each with a hue of their own. They illuminate complex textures of feeling in a manner that only one who has plunged to the depths and risen to the heights can envision. Each is a song— set free like Shiva's arrows arching the great divide and bridging gaps where language crystallizes glimpses of the infinite.

As I lay reading these poems, I felt I was glimpsing another planet surrounded by a bottomless sea of stars. Like the stars, our hearts are set ablaze by the nameless lights of the eternal, shared across the vast jeweled expanse. These poems speak from a shared longing. They are like swirling dervishes around an infinite source of divine light that we call SHIVA.

So, we drink from the same effulgent, timeless source of infinite splendor, returning us to the oneness. Transcending all barriers of time and space, this shared longing, through the spiral of words, carries us to the very source of wordless brilliance that lies in the center and holds it all together. The yearning for the grace of the divine, for our gurus, our benefactors, and ourselves, ultimately brings us full circle. It brings us to that very Shakti and Shiva, alive and at home in our hearts. It immerses us in the splendor of that which Pallavi does more justice than me in expressing since she is one privy to the murmuring gossip of the trees. Her roots entwined and connected through the soil of this earth, she has more than once read my mind. I recall one day as I walked through a field of scintillating light, the trees laughing as the sunshine and winds passing through their leaves. Suddenly, I received her text from India to California, "The trees have been gossiping all night here too!"

As shakti, she prods us to awaken, to pay attention, to be present when the sunshine in our hearts is revealed. She reminds us of that which perhaps has been forgotten or veiled by passing clouds. She invites us to remember and delight in the ultimate journey, bringing us full circle through the ever-deepening spirals of her poetry to the splendor within.

Knowing this, it is with humility that I take part in the unveiling of these poems. Please come along and enjoy this adventure, this festival of lights which makes each of our journeys brighter. May these poems find a place in your heart as they have.....in mine.

Kailasam Berke,
Long Beach, California,
May 28, 2017.

INDEX

AABHAR...GRATITUDE...The magic key to abundance.

VAIRAAGYA...The detached dispassion.

AMAVASYA... The dark night of the soul.

SHIVA& SHAKTI…The Amalgamation.

SAMPOORNA..The divine merger….A Global embracing.

GURU....The doorway to beyond.

The Witty Pied Piper

The Witty Pied Piper

I cringe at your touch,
My sores resurrected.
From their forgotten graves,
The ghosts of doom,
The demons of despair,
The Satan of melancholy,
All re birth at your beckoning.
I ask myself,
why did I
Surrender to thou?
Was it to bleed my heart thus?
And then;
you don on your flute,
And like **the witty pied piper**,
Lead my glooms to their demise.

Guru's Grace

Guru's Grace

The pinnacle of truth,
The archetype of compassion,
The succor of motherhood,
The strength of a father,
The bliss of a yogi,
The ecstasy of a lover,
The fountain head of creativity..
You are symbolic of all these.
All seeking retires at your lotus feet,
All strivings plain futility,
Where ought one go
When one has all ready arrived?

Playing with Thee.

If I win......Thou is mine.

If I lose....I am Thine.

Oh....what a game.

The Divine Prophesy

The Divine Prophesy

In the treacherous karma maze,
You come to light up paths.
Were it not for you,
I'd be unfound to grace.
"Guru", the dispeller of ignorance,
The master archer of destiny,
The ocean of compassion.
I offer at thy feet, my worthless ego,
Crush it under your mighty feet,
Demise my ignorance,
And birth me anew.
With surrender you say,
I can win,Let me master **this divine prophesy**

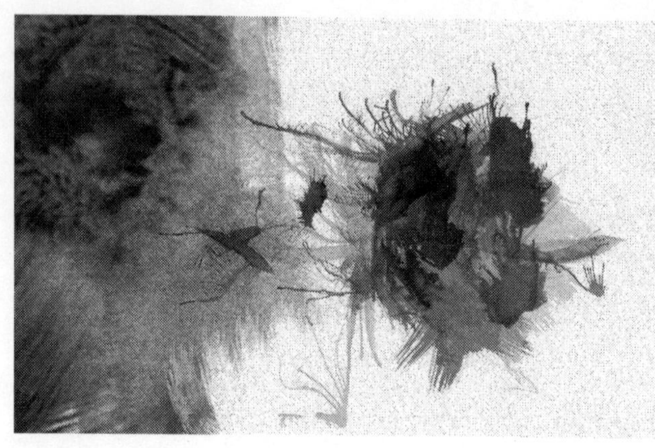

Guru..The Master Artist

Guru..The Master Artist

We assembled around you,A flock of thirsty seekers.
As everyone was in dynamic exchange,I was stoned
to your magnificent presence.
The delicacy of your eyes touching colors,
The beauty of your fingers,
Instilling life into paper forms.
Undivided attention to precision,
And yet, the flow of figurines so effortless.
Your fingers seemed to be God's very own.
Shaping, re molding our destiny patterns,
Burning out our effigies of pains, scars & failures,
The crimsons and purples of our auras
Scintillating in majestic fashions of the light.
Ah…the pristine healing moment,
Bursting in us divine ecstasy!
Can you sculpt me too, this similar fashion?
Until then, let me breathe your living grace.

The Awaited Transmutation

The Awaited Transmutation

This constant humming of a buzzing mind
Comes to a standstill halt at your lotus feet.
All remorse, worries and speculation meet no better demise
Than in your sacred waters.
The anguishes of guilt, the shadows of doubt,
Wade their way through me to reach your step
Where you sing hymns and chants to lull them to sleep.
I have been a thinker all along,
You teach me the essence of being.
I ask how can I be eternally grateful
And you birth to me infinite sleeping reasons.
I wonder what you do to my sorrow,
It shamelessly shuns even my shadows.
You remind me the essence of my soul self
Whose fragrance I have long ignored.
You embody to me self perfection in all its fullness
And warn me to lean on none.
You renew my self sufficiency and the illusory nature
Of my self portrayed poverty.
You memorize and repeat the truth of perennial change
Empowering by affirming that, "This too shall pass".

The pious ambience of your gaze
Makes me watch deeper where
I remain as my eternal self
Flowing and dancing to the ever dynamic "now".
Always loved, forever blessed, nirgun and pavitra,
With such beauty and tenderness,
You craft to me
My awaited transmutation

A Happier Me

A Happier Me

I come to you
draped in shadows of grey,
that percolate their roots deep.
You talk of colors,
I am nostalgic about their past presence.
Happiness happened eons away,
You claim every appearing moment to be joy.
I sing Looney tunes,
You are bliss in sheer symphony.
The darks are all I have known,
You narrate dreams of scintillating lights.
I stand desolate amidst the autumn,
you are the cherries and maples of spring.
I am a nonbeliever in relationships,
You endorse and affirm our eternal connections.
you forgive, correct and bless.
I know not optimum reciprocation,
My only offerings are my tears.
Is gratefulness only an asset of the brave and the capable
or worth has a weight to it?
Drenched in your surmounting compassion,
my soul hangs loosely and merrily.
in a zone of fearlessness,
freedom and gaiety,

I leave from you with a lighter step,
humming a happy tune.
now, I ought get used to
A Happier "ME"

The Timeless Grace

The Timeless Grace

You engulf me
Like the infinities of time,
Unto you,
I drown with hurried gurgles.
All my archetypes
Now turn vestigial.
You have scraped my past
And rewarded me no future.
So, here I am,
Sinking into your **timeless grace**

The Stupor Of Devotion

The Stupor Of Devotion

The world passes me by,
And I am barely aware.
The happenings of the days boast of their presence,
And yet, I lose all opportunity to condemn or praise.
What pathology could this be?
Indifference, disillusionment or depression
All claim their power equally on me.
Lost in the cacophony of these melodramatic tones,
I arrive at your step.
My mind is hungry for some petty gains.
Many speak high of your sacred place.
So, I come to you in curiosity and daze.
I sit before you, stoned to grace.
The eyes merely look,
The ears barely listen.
Your divine fervor has annihilated my senses.
All sorrows and anguish banished to hell.
Only the tears flow as remembrance of brevity.
I check to see my status update.
And then I know, the "I" is long ago dead,
And happily swallowed
by **the stupor of devotion**

The Supreme Liberation

The Supreme Liberation

When the pangs of worldly desires
have stopped ripping your heart apart,
and your wholeness is prostate
at the lotus feet of the Guru,
What force can devastate your piety?
Who can snatch away your zeal?
The only qualification is the unconditional devotion
that blows up your ego to minces.
Oh! my beloved master,
grant me **this supreme liberation**

The Celebration

The Celebration

In the solitary confines
of my ordinary life,
There occurs a sporadic miracle
that never had been before.
When the "I" in me is in slumber,
And worries lurk a mile away,
You arrive at the gateway of my higher self.
In glittering gold, you adorn and pride,
Your aura, a lightning of super bliss,
Melodies of light on your smiling face,
Seize my wrinkles of older lifetimes.
Lyrics of gaiety flood my heart,
and bring me to sing from a muted voice.
All in me is a 'brand new',
no traces of the phantom, old.
You glance at my shackled feet,
and split open these ancient chains.
I arise from my seat of sorrows,
and then I no more , rest or sleep.
We dance & frolick
in your ocean of compassion.
the Gods gaze down upon on us,
in awe and jealous admiration
to testimony my anointed birth
in the embrace of this **celebration**

The allegorical presentation
far more reaching, revealing,
than the precise dictates.
For, it is in getting lost, erased,
which is the arrival.
Not in the reaching
of a defined destination.

The Pursuit

The Pursuit

In the dreams of mystical orchards,
May I not be lost.
In the ego's ambition of siddhis,
May I not get embroiled.
In the anatomy of rites and rituals,
May I remain simple and devoted.
In the valleys of sorrows and grief,
May the suns of hope always rise,
In the pursuit of success and glamour,
May I remain in centered humility,
All I seek is a corner in the vision of your grace.
And single pointed devotion to thee.
My worlds know of not a better **pursuit**

The Sacred Homage

The Sacred Homage

I come to thee…soiled & broken,
A muddle head of confusions,
A spring of sorrow,

Happiness was in jeopardy,
And life; a torment to bear.
My beliefs were contaminated,
And my heart in turmoil.
Your presence soothed,
You anointed my wounds,

Now, I know not all was in vain,
like tiny dew drops that fell on the parch,
I absorbed and sipped on this elixir,
rejuvenation came in showers sometimes,
and at others, as realizations that ached.
all I welcomed as divine grace.

The cells sparkling,
The eyes dancing,
I landed at your doorstep, new & alive,
Who would know what has changed
other than you who had started it all.
In silence & in your words,

The weary soul revived to love,
How you managed to hear the whispers
that had barely escaped my heart.
The goose bumps of awe,
The tears of gratitude,
The pangs of devotion,
The offerings of realizations,
The climax of actions,
The perils of transformation,
All these, I offer at your lotus feet,
I know not what to do with these treasures
that spill out of me at every contact.
Allow me pride at least a while
to be worthy of your blessed & loved.

The Righteous Consummation

The Righteous Consummation

In the lap of your divine grace,
I come to recluse in the self.
Thirsty for thy nectarine benevolence,
I stand quenched in delight.
All aspirations, ambitions and desire
Transmute on exposure to your wisdom infinite.
I sip on this elixir drop by drop
And get wealthy with this sacred nourishment.
Delusions and illusions stand at thy pronouncement
The will of evil cries aloft at thy lofty predicament
And all I hear are hymns of bliss.
Illumination must surely mimic your eyes
As they fix themselves on me.
The descent of the mind from royal chariots
Into the humble abode of my heart.
A soundless journey that explodes with the light
This pious merger is both the means and the end
As the "I" in me has encountered
Its
Righteous consummation

The Meal

The Meal

At the table
Me and my guru
Sat to eat.
Much was served..
Joy, pain and the like.
I desired to eat.
He did not allow...
In a moment of obedience
The plates were empty.
He had gobbled it all.
No one remained in me to crave....

Krishna...The Enigma

Krishna...The Enigma

In the change of spectacles, we have a fresh insight
twisters to the brain the heart full of delight.
a single one… completely complete.
and yet, a mirage to the un awakened one.
Myriads to offer to each one of us,
in forms that we are attuned to see.
He is the regulator of the universal plan
a mischievous toddler, anchored in strength.
an erotic archetype that spells lust,
a devotee personified, a master in disguise.
a king maker, brings the flute to life
so many persons and yet never personified.
profane desires alternating with immense control,
This world… his matchless maaya
where he keeps us magically enthralled
shows us glimpses, then disappears,
Our devotion, the best guide
to unlock this Pandora box of moksha.
His leela, an eternal celebration,
of a life lived in freedom and intensity,
Lets rejoice to his anointed birth.

Prema..The Rewarding Paradox

The Divine Prostration

The Divine Prostration

In the concealment of this newness,
Is a vision ancient and old.
In shadows of sorrow,
Burst forth sporadic volcanoes of the light.
One may have never known,
And yet be intimately close.
Through these familiar paths,
Flow nascent rivers of truth.
The murmur is most often of love
When words are sparingly used.
Awaken, bow and surrender
To the mightiness of love.
Nothing else is more worthy
Of your **divine prostration**

The Ordained Inception

The Ordained Inception

Through forbidden boundaries
You sneak unto my private zones,
Through the deepest woods,
You trail to conquer my heart's fortress.
I had appropriately misplaced myself
Love found me unalarmed, yet again.
I had sat sulking in absence,
You arrive like ethereal presence.
In a doubtless fashion
You invade my unseen shell
And bring me to compose a matrix of words.
Creativity has much in common
With the way of procreation.
Both know well the adamant routes
They cause one to swell and swell
Until one has been victimized
By an **ordained inception**

The Distant Relations

The Distant Relations

On a certain ordinary day,
When the world happens to fade
Against the background of one's melancholy moods,
The sight becomes a vacant stare.
Love merely a fairy tale,
One's mind only brave enough to persevere
In the facades of life's drama,
All players have played their part,
Only I remain on the empty stage.
Accompanied by the glaring myth of it all.
Chilling my spine to the eerie loneliness,
I wish for at least a single companion.
And all I find is, deserted & dark.
Ah! Where can I rest a while?
And be embraced in love & care?
I need to be loved
Even if it be the greatest myth.
At least a while,
Until I stumble
My way back home.

The Sacred Copulation

The Sacred Copulation

The voids in me seek a companion,
Is complimentation an avalaible option?
the 'I' in me has been ripped away,
then whose is this desire for communion?
days at end, I maze in solitary enigmas,
The mirages of love continue to haunt.
I know now for sure of love as a myth.
Yet, why the turn around and tug?
I gave up on these long ago.
I'm not sterile, neither impotent.
Desire is what fails me often,
Would my life exemplify some novice pattern?
And am I worthy of a blessed reproduction?
In me, truth will take on a new life.
My womb has ached for this across lifetimes.
Now, I have finally learnt reception
In the classrooms of devotion.
Will I be a worthy participant
In this **sacred copulation**

The Divine Amalgamation

The Divine Amalgamation

On my seeking journey,
Every few miles, I encounter love, my holy friend.
Who spreads before me a sacred road map.
He has his unique ways to teach,
A style that signatures with tears.
I never mind learning from love,
Coz he does it with care.
Sometimes strange lessons unfold
In the classrooms of love
Where the seeker and the sought
Merge in **divine amalgamation**

Love through sight is of the perishable.

There is a Love whose touch.....immortalizes.

This touch does not use the sensory structure...either to flow ...or to receive.

The language of Love is not in time.

There is a Love....whose touch immortalizes.

The Participants

The Participants

When words cease to travel between us,
When the breath no longer scents,
When the beats no longer boom,
When bodies lie separated by time,
And souls ache to pungent sorrows,
In this paused timelessness,
In this quantum void,
There occurs a mystic communication
Which no longer leans on presence.
It has its own ways,
An intelligence beyond compare.
It questions and replies
Both at once.
Embalms and caresses,
It is crispy in humor,
Bursting with wisdom.
The intellect merely a lost army,
Love, the master archer!
In this surrendered silence,
We stand as mere **participants**

The Overflowing Renaissance

The Overflowing Renaissance

When the early showers
Sprinkle us with glimpses of love,
The heart is awakened from a slumber deep.
Aches of older lifetimes echo in response.
Will it be more real this time?
Will it last?
Shadows of lust overhangs
A dense matrix of emotions.
Are we meant for time togetherness
Or are we mere co travelers?
I find myself crushed
Under this melodramatic avalanche.
Soaked in overflowing desire,
I lust.....once again
To be in the majestic presence of love!
The heart is a freelancing traveler
It knows no fear or loss.
My only conditioning ought be
A deep surrender to it all.
Under its huge umbrella,
I find myself virgin, yet again
To this **overflowing renaissance**

The Concealment

The Concealment

They say love is eternal,
and one may be obliged to believe,
lovers have a sense of frenzied intensity
that could change equations of love,
In a heightened awareness to the
Imperennial nature of love,
I happen to enter it, yet again.
having got the final verdict on love,
It once again threw its gates open to me,
the myth of love is clear & un debatable
only a broken heart will know.
however there could be a fair chance,
that even when presence fades,
love becomes a fragment of the mystic matrix,
as love needs not our physical presence,
consent or more,
eternal & yet so temporal is this love,
In the universal database,
every love remains etched
in a divine encoded **concealment**

The Sacred Intimacy

The Sacred Intimacy

The night has passed between us...
Leftover of love remain.
The passion has drowned
After an observation deep;
And we have drunk
From each other's eyes a bit too much.
This makes my head dizzy
And has left my soul too wet.
How much will u worship me?
I am mere mortal....
Only before you
I turn into a Love Goddess...
Bring me to you
And lie in me deep.
In this **sacred intimacy**
Let us be born
Yet again....

The New Found Love

The New Found Love

I have been wet in my soul
And pleased in the body...
In the drenching of delight
I have discovered myself anew.
And polished by passion,
I ravish a new flavor
where my soul and mind have
Leaped over on its fences
To peep into a magical world.
Here pleasure resides at heart
And the hurries are long forgotten.
The sunshine is delicious
As it gently alights at my parched skin.
The springs of ecstasy
Break free from the cracks
of the luminescent soils.
You and me hang around
Lazily entwined on tree top branches
Exchanging silent passion on our lips.
The body is mere medium,
You romance my soul ..
In a stupor twang
we exchange slurred love notes..
We become protagonists

of a dynamic freedom that had tricked us so far.
Our spins slowing, our breath at hang,
We awaken to our new forms.
You worship me with your passion
I succumb and bless you back.
The shame shunned like never before,
In all nakedness of spirit,
We commune into
Our **new-found love**

The Anticipations

The Anticipations

The tendrils of jasmine
Have wrapped themselves around me
And leave only my curves to bare.
This moon has become too shameless
And started to peep from the clouds.
These linen on which I laze
Are soaked with my wet longings,
And the anxieties of communion
Keep sleep away from my eyes.
This night has been a long one
submerging me unto it.
The skin is warm and flushed,
The breath a tandem faster,
The heart a beat amiss,
The groins are at fire.
Through the maze of my fuzzy thoughts
I hear you calling my name...
Where shall I hide
From the intensity of you
Lest we burn to it alive...

The Impending Meeting

The Impending Meeting

A recommended way
Is to stay in the now.
And yet you snatch me
From the pangs of time
To plant me close to you.
In gardens of sheer delight
Where the hearts are in full bloom
And tuck at each other's strings,
Where words have become amnesic
And every relay occurs
Only Though glance and touch..
In these stilled spaces,
We will nestle unto a corner
Where the world has forgotten to witness.
In these misplaced zones
We can be fully present
To each other's arrival
In a naked and honest way.
You, me and the silence between us
Hustled and cocooned in the
Womb of our deep intimacy.
Nothing remains a pursuit,
We only dare to BE...
WITNESS to our **impending meeting**

Vectors Of Singularity

Vectors Of Singularity

You seem nascent and unaware
To my passionate tides.
In your subtle knowingness
And in my innocent advances,
We slowly progress towards our communion.
You raise yourself a bit,
I lift myself to you.
You lie low, I lie below you.
In either ways,
Our geometry
Is always complimentary
To our deepest intimacy possible.
When the breath between us has faded,
And the bodies know no shame,
The overlap is not physical mere,
the souls have entwined to love.
We stand testament to being
Vectors of singularity

The Love Communion

The Love Communion

Shed the mundane formalities of speech,
gaze at the soul that transcends the eyes.
shun all formalities of knowledge
and walk me to the vast infinite..
Here the suns are many and ignited,
The moons simmer at the muddy banks.
on the ice of this corroded surface,
breaths the slow fire of desire.
I beckon at you with open arms
to come and share the delight of intimacy.
Here… life sips on its unending ecstasy.
Passion is a thimble feel
when one is gulping on waterfalls of lust.
Soak every way that you know of,
and yet, the source is undiminished.
We are separated by our bodies nude,
what good are they to serve us now
when the souls dance to a merry celebration
of our heightened **love communion**

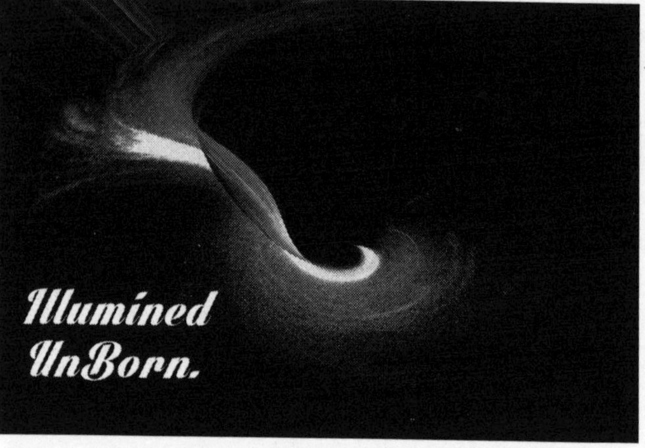

The Morning Stars

The Morning Stars

Most is known about their special sparkle,
and the way they ignite the skies.
On cloudy nights, they are deeply missed,
with the moon, they share deep ties.
At break of day, easily forgotten
their purpose as hidden as them.
One may doubt whether they even exist.
You and I are like **the morning stars**

Adieu My Love

Adieu My Love

You are with me, and yet someone so new,
What broke you up and left you less than few?
You pain seems higher than what seems right,
You succumb to the shadows which I know not how
to fight.
Your need for space has engulfed my whole being,
The only way left is to just stop trying.
You wander amongst the virtual, denying us our love,
however gloomy it looks, it's only a shadow above.
Pardon me my impatience for I know not how to
wait,
for you return from the corpses and kneel at my
heart's gate.
Though I love you intense, our love has fallen apart,
It cannot bridge the few steps that lead unto my
heart.
My poems no longer bleed you, nor tear your eyes
with dew,
Still, I'll try a last time, with words that sound few.
Come to me when you complete the rituals of
remorse and
worry,
I hope it's not too late and I wish I don't make you
hurry.

Shoonya: The timeless now… A dwelling place

The Journey

The Journey

In the cause less chaos,
of Alternating frenzy and sedation,
I take upon a **journey**
That returns me to myself.
It seems quite a long mile,
And an arduous uphill trail.
I close my eyes to sigh,
And breathe a little more air.
An awakening from this
Soon finds me home....

The Martyr

The Martyr

This overhanging night of dilemmas,
This overtly delayed dawn,
must hold a sure message for me.
I witness from my window,
the hesitant rain plunging into the silent still of the night.
makes me wonder what holds it back.
distraught and disappointed is my search,
Is there a destination that
awaits my failing steps?
Is time challenging my gut
or is it mere a threatening illusion?
So succumbing is this inertia
and yet so real, its feel.
One might regret the weary long travel
when the arrival is all ready proclaimed.
Singing joyous tunes,
with poems on my lips,
I dance in celebration of this moment.
Let me challenge the dawn
by the dagger of my darkness
It is not always with the light
that power ought reside.
I race to nowhere,
I seek no refuge,
I'd rather die as a
martyr to the now.

An Appointment With Time

An Appointment With Time

Travelling across lifetimes,
I spot varying destinations.
I engage in experiences.
I hiccup with ecstasy.
the gamut of phenomena,
the cacophony of the mind,
constant companions on a mystical journey!
Cracking karmic mazes seems no ordinary fate.
Is saadhna the answer
or grace my recluse?
Is enlightenment a journey
or a pin point destination?
the bliss of a yogi,
the love of a sufi,
the enquiry of gyaana,
or the mires of service and action.
Self realization has so many shades,
I taste a bit of each.
but am full of none of them.
My intuitiveness shocks me sometimes,
My intellect , a paranoia,
I see saw on this long…
and seek respite from it all.
The ramifications of identity

crawl and coil over the real 'me'.
with Guru's grace, I experience surrender.
and a freedom infinite.
now, I move freely across dimensions.
light in my heart, joyful in my step,
the past is redundant,
the future unwilling to worry.
what option there is other than "the now"?
Timelessness is larger and vaster,
Time, merely a built illusion.
My myth has been shattered
of **an appointment with time**

The Merry Cloud

The Merry Cloud

In a sky infinite,
Whose seams burst at its horizon,
And carvings of infinite forms
Struggle to make felt their splendor,
Night and day differently abled,
Depictions of beauty pristine.
Galaxies bursting with quantum truths,
Amidst the darker voids,
Here I am!
The tiny me, lingering on.
Splitting open my presence
To infinite grace.
Why ought I have form,
Or mind, reason or color
When the patron of the sky
allows me freedom of expression?
So, I'll just rejoice in this eternal moment
Where I am
Endless, colorless, formless, mindless,
A merry cloud
basking in the light.

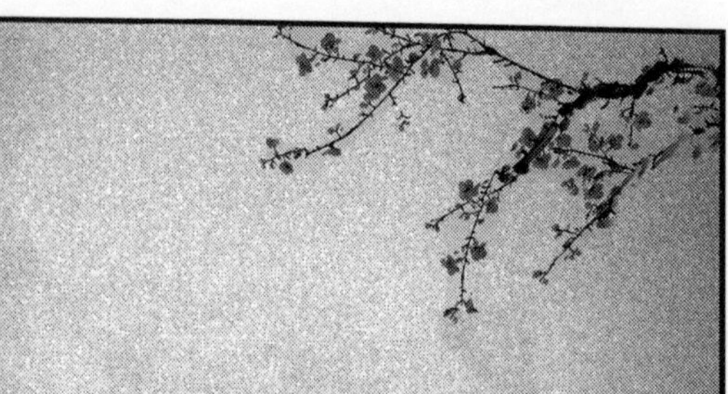

Time has no hold
on what thought has not constructed.

The Timelessness of Remembrance

The Timelessness of Rememberance

All rituals of devotion,
All sermons of wisdom,
All disciplines of worship
Have known extinction in me.
Sometimes I wonder if I have turned agnostic
Or maybe true grace has befallen me.
Anytime, anywhere, any day
Is the perfect way to be.
The only gauge of surrender
Are the tears that salt my soul.
All mentions of your name
Take me beyond the horizons
Into the **timelessness of remembrance**

Be Nothing

Be Nothing

I'll come to you
When you tire from all efforts
And lie in abandon
With outstretched hands
To watch the infinite sky
Sparkling back at you...
There will be silence
And acceptance in your eyes
As I lie beside, mimicking God...
You will be low
I will be lower;
And yet when we commune,
the skies will only be the limit..
When a tear will touch your soul,
I will drink from its depths.
When laughter brims your eyes,
My heart will hold a cup.
When you will know sorrow,
I'll lease your memory to hell.
When you will **become a nothing**
I'll engulf you unto me...

The Misty Wanderlusts

The Misty Wanderlusts

My thirsty eyes
Have cracked open to arid winds
That blow from faraway lands.
My supper lies cold before me
And the hunger has been long absent.
All tools of transformation
Are restless to bring about change;
But I stand in tsunamis of preordained destiny.
Where are the blinking stars
That were once upon lighthouses?
Direction remains unknown,
Only the journey prevails.
However there is abandon
And freedom from all worry.
Only an ecstasy prevails
That swallows its own wounds..
In this timeless travel
through euphoric galaxies...
I slip on and on
Towards my **misty wanderlusts**

The Misplaced Tavern

The Misplaced Tavern

I and you
In the lap of a beautiful dream.
I sing for you..you dance for me.
The left over wine in the cups
drooling with the ecstasy of our lips upon them.
We can neither sleep, nor lie awake.
Inebriated with a divine hangover.
Lust has now given up on us,
Only love rides high. Intoxicated fervor,
And the nakedness of truth.
No distances separate the bodies and mind...
You are all raw
And I have lost my shame.
We exchange turns
To peak to holy orgasms..
The infinities lie aghast
At such a careless spill ...
Pray...Who will lead us home
From this **misplaced tavern**

Samarpan: Surrender...A Way of Being

I get nothing by being fragnant.
I am just helpless
to be otherwise.

Twilight Tutorials

Twilight Tutorials

At twilight hour,
Lessons come flooding to me.
Darkness has no identity of its own,
It's merely the lack of light.
All beauty is transient,
Only the truth prevails.
Just like the crimsons, indigos and oranges pale,
Yet, the sky remains the same.
Why do we need greatness, might or success
When splendor & beauty rain their grace
Limitlessly on our pristine self?
Why, who, where, when? all these questions only lead inward.
In silence, all is answered
And one can just be…

The Dynamics Of Surrender

The Dynamics Of Surrender

I was always a proponent
Of hard work and striving,
Until when it came to me
That destiny is about acceptance.
Love & joy can't be earned,
They come when one is unadorned.
Seeking merely is a placebo,
The only requirement is to be in the flow.
Gratitude only invites abundance,
Devotion is the right correspondence.
Surrender is the key to more and more,
Which is what needs the implore.
Sacred surrender works in dynamic ways,
Uncovering prosperity that dormant lays
So, seek no more, only believe,
& then sit back in patience to receive.

The Permission

The Permission

In the sacred sanctity of the self,
I come to recline & rest.
In the healing silence,
all pains numbed.
All joys revived.
Reconstructions,
Remodeling,
Realizations,
There's so much work happening;
While all I do is ALLOW...

The Infallible Self

The Infallible Self

Who do I belong to?
What is my place?
What am I seeking ?
and who is my solace?
Turning points at every step,
Decisions at every crossroad.
Life seems to be in a tearing hurry
Of what could be a timely discovery.
Why can't we accept unanswered questions?
or just stay blessed without any notions?
Is it mandatory to anchor in belief,
when one could just float without any grief?
Why should lyrics adorn all songs?
and rightfulness correct all wrongs?
The mind is averse to taking a "thought vacation",
all these flings cause only more sedation.
'Becoming' seems so much more important than
'being',
Isn't wisdom more important than mere knowing?
The rebel in me has thrown up a coup,
and now it seeks only to undo
the shackles that bind my limitlessness,
and bring forth the glory of
the Infallible self

The Epoch

The Epoch

The prairies of darkness
Rebel against the seams of horizons,
The memoirs of lifetimes
Ache as if denuded, yet again.
The wraths of insult
Demolish all regard.
The blizzards of despair
Blow at the soul's windowsill.
We must be warriors,
Or devotees; at least.
This **epoch** of life
Must find its way through us,
To be kissed by the light
Until
Each of these ammunitions
Lose their adorn on us.
And all we are left with
Is the presence of an engulfing silence,
A non judgmental freedom
That we are truly deserving of.

The Rightful Place

The Rightful Place

Bewitched by the resplendent moonlight,
sparked by the dazzling sun,
the flowers intoxicating me with fragrance,
the majestic mountains crashing my ego,
and the infinities of the skies belittled my pride,
the ecosystem with its matchless intelligence
has disgraced what is termed, "human super
evolution".
With so much to wrong my delusions of grandeur,
in slow surrender,
I know
my **rightful place**

The Ambience of Life

The Ambience of Life

Verily this life of mine
Must be more than mere breath.
So, I made myself more important
By surrounding myself with purpose.
There was much to fulfill,
Such less as a lifetime.
Portraits of myself
In shades of all sorts.
Wow, I really had so much
That my life could boast of.
The parodies of successes,
The pursuits of knowledge
were so much reason to live.
And then one day, sitting beneath a tree
Basking in its succor and shade,
I saw it brim with flowers and fruits.
Yet, there was no pride,
In fact, Not even purpose.
Life is its own purpose.
The rest is merely **ambience to life**

No experience .....anchoring itself...
...in a....meaning...
....whether it is the experience of birth...
...or of death...
...or of the brief interval in-between...

....one is.

The Denied Flowering

The Denied Flowering

Fullness must also begin
With a nascent seed.
It has no insignia
Without the touch of grace.
I might be thimble,
Yet I have managed unto the now.
With a rustic sophistication,
A gullible form,
There is beauty rigged in bits of me...
That the grace has faithfully enshrined..
I am naive and juvenile,
Yet..Transparent like a sieve.
No color has touched me,
No impressions have taint,
I belong only to love....
In my being so,
I have refuted fruition
To prevail as the innocent one...
I revere and rejoice
In my **denied flowering**

DRISHTA : WITNESSING... Educating the self.

The Retreat

The Retreat

Lots is happening at my end,
Every happening another step
To lead me to stillness and bliss.
All that's wane & external
Fades away like lighter cloud.
Residues of nostalgias
Surface once in a while.
Like waves, they rise
Only to fall back in the ocean's lap.
Observing is what leads me further,
Knowing has fewer implications,
Flowing means much much more.
The arrogance of personalities
Are sights that pass me by.
All one ought do, is remain & watch.
Compassion, a mistaken instrument of the ego,
Service only to gather gains,
Judgments float around
While the key is only to accept.
The easier is discarded,
The complex, worshipped.
Agony and bliss are both sights,
Both make their own impressions,
On those who are willing to bear their cross.
I am in search of freedom

From identities, strategies and titles,
Travelled too far on these paths,
And now retreating to the universal self.

The Justified Incarnation

The Justified Incarnation

Transient satisfactions, the squeal of success,
Desires incarnated and translated to achievements,
The treadmills of daily mundane demands,
The obedience of social structures,
A race without a needed pause,
The trivial journey of life,
Often masked by worldly ways
Seeks to entail on an inner quest.
A longing that welcomes one home
And unveils life's divine purpose.
Through a ripened reflection,
Transcending biological reaction,
A utopian matrix of mystic imagination,
The self and its contemplation,
Are all ambience
Of a **justified incarnation**

Witnessing

The Dispassionate Witnessing

In the zones of receding senses,
When one is purely 'aware',
One travels to enigmatic zones
Which are boundless & vast.
This place is sacredness,
Where entry is denied
To those who don't know stillness.
In a surrendered awareness,
Where the mind has been emptied of all debate,
Where all cloaks of conditionings
And the paraphernalia of dialogue
Has been shamelessly shunned,
I escape into this silent zone.
Here, God, me & existence
Have overlapping boundaries.
Only a **dispassionate witnessing** prevails.

The Gaieties of Life

The Gaieties of Life

All days are bursting with magic
Only if we see them so.
Where is all this brimming from,
And who regulates the flow?
The birds seem ecstatic and free,
Who taught the trees to swoon?
Rainbows spill with colors,
And the caterpillars to groom.
Water flows of its own accord,
The clouds hurry past.
Oceans rage with unlimited waves,
Yet, still at their heart of heart.
Spiders busy knitting their webs,
Predators at their pry.
Only humans seem not to notice,
Anything other than their own cry.
The majesty of planets,
The crowning of new constellations.
Down comes the rainfall,
And higher peak, the mountains.
Why is so much hurry and worry
When all is in perfect time?
We just need to recline in rest
And let our worlds shine.

Very unwanted is this strife,
When we are blessed with **the gaieties of life**

Life gave.

Life took.

I am

The Stoic

The Stoic

One may roll over all one's sides,
and yet, find not exceptions any!
The autumn winds rob
the structures of majestic trees,
The springs then come,
adding novelty and green.
Celebrations of birth,
The midways of sufferings and joys,
Life unfolds an array of experiences,
until the curtains draw a close at death.
Lilies, roses and the like
bloom to simmering beauty
Soon, meet their demise.
The planets, black holes and meteors,
All are subject to changing course.
No thought is steady,
No emotion un labile.
This fleeting panorama
of cyclical fates…Ah!!
I thought I could rest a while,
only to know the myth of it all.
Karma constantly operates on us.
"transformation" is the perennial word,
"change", the only ethical vogue.
to witness these with a steady eye
is the gleeful & courageous **stoic's way**

One has never moved out of the now.
Never.
Ever.
One has never been in the now.
Ever.

Be

Be

When the edge of time announces its termination,
There is a majestic herald of an enlarging void,
In meditative trance or a single moment of bhakti,
We are consented to touch this realm
Where all sense of doing retires to the backseat
Only allowing remains as perfect qualification.
In this pious dimension,
all conditionings experience a drop out,
Even the task of observation fades,
The duality of prayer is effortlessly transcended
And one can joyfully **be**

The Holon

The Holon

One within another
And yet a distance apart,
Like a paradox that prevails
Denying phantoms of duality,
A rebel that is structured and in absolute freedom.
Contemplating on its own thought
And yet building segments of plans,
Midway between life and death
This existence just floats..
I AM
The holon

The Sukshma

The Sukshma

In the pulsating tenderness of being,
I have come to alight
On a hidden perch..
Where the hurts have all been seized,
the sorrows vaporizing to
A million suns ..
There s balm on the heart,
ecstacy in spirit.
Your tinkle of laughter,
Has left me a little frenzied
And given me a niche
Where I can dare to belong.
And yet know that none
Of it is mine..
This magnanimity of spirit
Has flooded me with gratitude
That ripples on the surface
And the bed still remains still...
Like the dust motes
That oscillate in the scintillating beams,
I have come to reverberate
And rejoice to my being.
Now;
I have come to become
The sukshma

The Dark Colored Ecstasy

The Dark Colored Ecstasy

Where's my form?
Had it just a while ago...
Where's my mind?
Submerged in a void of thoughts....
Where's my heart?
Weary of the aches of love...
Where are my possessions?
That Don't charm me to joy...
Where's my life?
All Blended into the global...
Flashes of illumination
Are ancient and obsolete..
With no one to be
And nowhere to go...
I am in a new reverie
Of my
Dark coloured ecstacy

The Vanishing

The Vanishing

As spring overtakes winter,
And autumn robs the bejeweled trees,
The earth on a perennial spin ,
And the universe fluxes to its dynamic states,
wrinkles arrive on a senile face,
And the flowers demise after a radiant Bloom,
Death and life in an endless row,
Love and loss in a follow suit,
Why would enlightenment be spared
Of a subtleness and spontaneity?
Most evolvement makes no noise
and gracefully finds its prevailing course.
Only the human mind is full of fathom
Of the presence of a grand unveiling.
It must now shun this care..
Like the blossoming that brings to rendition
The image of beauty and grace,
I'll lose my density
By the day
And silently **vanish** to thin air..

AABHAR...

GRATITUDE...The magic key to abundance.

Absence to Presence

Absence to Presence

When one has been taught
How to live on the edge,
The corners seem cozy & warm.
When one has known the infinity of sorrow,
Laughter is possible on mundane jokes.
When one has known a day's starvation,
One can be grateful for a plate full.
When one has seen sickness come alive,
Life's dances are merrier than more.
When one has known the pangs of solitude,
Gatherings are welcome and in store.
What else is there to feel and know,
Other than our"breath" which we just took?
It is surely the biggest gift.

The Grateful Prayer

The Grateful Prayer

As the sleepy percussions,
Lost hold on me this morning
And I sat in wonder
What would be my grateful prayer
There proclaimed through a peep in the window,
A beautiful ray of light
with the assets of the
infinities dancing in them..

The Sacred Ritual

The Sacred Ritual

Tonight, my poverty is a great bliss.
The lamps burn on leftover oils,
My pet dozes over an empty bowl,
The moon in a lazy recline,
Aching men drowned in their blessed slumbers,
I'm grateful for this forgiving solitude
Which allows me privacy
For the **sacred ritual** of tears.

The Sailing

The Sailing

At the harbor of enlightenment,
Lie the coffins of our identities,
The setting suns, being reminders
Of our predicaments, our sins.
Twilight zones fading fast,
All knowing and learnt lessons,
Dissolving to a huge void.
Our gurus, our lighthouses,
Steering us in perfect direction and speed,
We have known love, loss and more.
Now, it's time we undo our anchor,
And set sail to uncharted lands,
We are never alone,
We are always free,
We are super blessed,
May we never return!

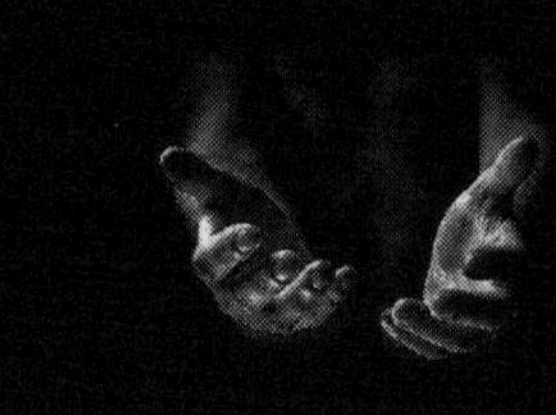

A reaching for oneself.

The Challenge

The Challenge

Today, I will do some aware sun gazing,
A little peeping into an inviting nest,
The flowers, a little more appreciated,
The river bank, more sat upon,
Through busy days,
I'll dare to dream,
Through sleepy nights,
I'll wake to cry.
Tiny pats on children's backs,
Little unannounced acts of charity.
Laughter spells on futile jokes,
Cringes of anger on tiny matters,
Why can't I live to the fullest,
The changing shades of my heart?
Today, I'll truly give **challenge**
To the life
I belong to.

The Healer

The Healer

I know of pills and elixirs many,
many a men visit me daily.
I treat and embalm with hands and heart.
Sometimes, the heart palpates their pain
that ache in their souls so bruised.
What could I do better?
this always spurs my seek.
and then it hits in the next moment,
Who are" you" to do?
and how can you be better than the best?
Heal your arrogance and give up doer ship.
The attitude of service is also a morphed ego pursuit.
A good intent
and a healing heart
is enough to light up an ailing soul.
The rest are his blessings and love
which I humbly mimic of.

The Ancient Spiral

The Ancient Spiral

Fractals of light,
Carved by architects of consciousness,
Etched in every miniscule corner,
Endorsing the equanimity of all existence.
Galaxies in universes,
The crawling snails,
Seahorse's tails,
The rising Kundalini,
And DNA of chromosomes,
All are woven in similar fashion,
They are foundations of the super creation.
I crawl out of sleep to a brand new awareness
To witness this **ancient spiral**

The Invitation

The Invitation

Mushrooms of joy,
Transplanted into my gardens,
Lilies of laughter
Rebelling through the cracks.
Songs of innocence
That challenge the mundane.
Dances of divine ecstasy
Throwing me off guard.
What exactly am I In my little bundle
With all my accompanying harem?
I am,
An **invitation** to the divine…

Well Earned Blessings

Well Earned Blessings

When a innocent bird
Holding a twig in its perch
Looks upon the sky
With an eye of delight and awe
In anticipation of the showers of grace upon it,
A sky of blessings cannot be denied
To this heart of gold....
It's not in the power of any
God to refuse Its hands to go up in blessing
When one has cleansed one's mirror well
And made a sacred altar
In the midst of his sullied heart.
A blessing is well earned
By a heart that thrives on its blood...

VAIRAAGYA... The Detached Dispassion.

The Last Leaf

The Last Leaf

As the mighty oak
Entered the blizzards of solemn winters,
It still retained a little age old glory.
It still had a pride
Of never ever succumbing.
As the chill deepened,
Much of it was lost to time and space.
Hope and faith however kept it on.
Most flowers and fruits had become vestigial,
The leaves slowly wilting away.
A lone last leaf held its reins.
On a rather more than beautiful day,
When the world was engaged with itself,
The last leaf broke all its promises
And floated gleefully away, away, away..
What remained, only the mighty oak knew,
In divine abandon, it had stilled itself to truth.

The Widowed Ego

The Widowed Ego

On the voyage of truth,
I set forth, my sail a mast.
You gift me oars,
And terminate all safe harbor.
The world fades at the the faraway horizon,
The dusk of dispassion colors my sky,
In the infinite oblivion,
I still to all pace.
The stars are above me,
The ocean below.
In this affirming absence,
All of me loses form.
My ego stands widowed from me,
And in this abandonment,
I celebrate!

The Dispassionate Mind

The Dispassionate Mind

The facets of complexities,
The facades of illusions,
The panoramas of ignorant chatters,
The whims of passionate desires,
The gamut of memoirs,
A well enacted drama of mirages,
The split spill of a schizophrenic mind!
The manias of ownership,
The egos of personalities,
Here, lies a tricky maze.
A dispassionate mind
However knows well
How to shun such illusions.

The Corpse

The corpse

In the midst of the day's pounding,
I sneaked into the caves of stillness.
with the darkness smoldering over me, thick,
I toppled over some rock like thing.
a tweak of light alighted on this stony **corpse.**
and guess what, it was a mutilated body
that had my very own face.
Taken aback, I stood there longer
to witness it with dispassionate sternness.
It bred in it the maggots of my past,
The knotted reminiscences of a time gone by,
Some of the body ruptured by disease,
Most of it, seared with scars.
I was clearly unidentifiable.
and then came an awakening deep.
that was indeed "my" dead corpse.
and behold....I looked at the living 'me'.
I was a scintillating being
flavored by a divine sacredness.
My humaneness alive & resplendent.
My smiling face, an angel's envy,
I had been remodeled by the light.
and had been granted
a long begged boon.
I was dead right in the midst of life.

The Sojourn

The sojourn

In songs of native origin,
Words are of least emphasis.
Riding high on waves of intuition
One could even fly to the poles.
The Christopher's map is ever guiding
To a nascent wanderer at sea.
What use is of anything, but love
In sealing the cracks of a fragmenting soul?
Ejection of gluttony woes,
Sarcasm of wicked flamboyant,
What use does bravery serve
When death has traced you to where you sleep?
Strategies of a fickle mind,
Compulsions of a hungry soul,
Make no stark difference to me.
I prevail....only with myself.
Just a little more,
And then, I'll herald
Another brand new **sojourn**

The Virile Existence

The virile existence

In the panoramic maze of life,
sequential patterns of karmic repeats,
coupled with the mounting dispassion to it all,
No respite from the sequel of fate,
bounding dooms of heightened expectations,
My fragility stands at the brink of retire.
My sensitivities numbed to doom,
Where ought one stay unharmed
when one is at the core of chaos?
I seek to retire from it all
and in a silence serene,
reassure myself of my eternal connections,
rest in the tranquility of the self,
and be aware and reminded of
my untainted soul
that remains untouched
by the **virility of my existence**

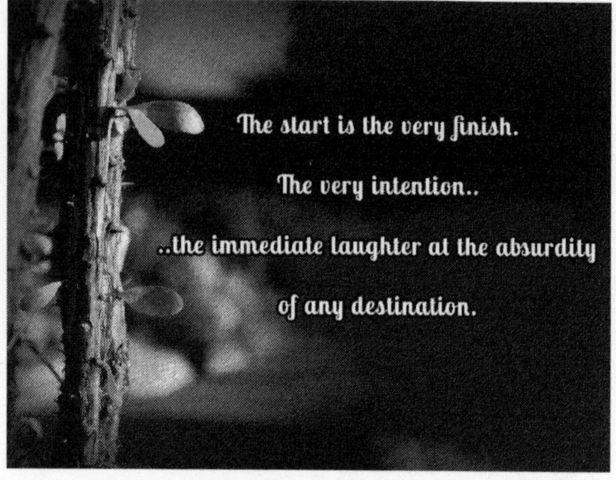

The Absurdity Of Destination

The absurdity of destination

This travel across lifetimes,
The race of arrival,
The exhilaration of success,
What does this account for?
Other than a narrative of the ego
Which takes a turn to pride
At its naive accomplishments....
I am too stunned to move
From the lap of this grace
And wade my way through the maze.
This ecstasy has robbed me of all ambition
And sufficed me to my brim.
In all divine satiety
And a fulfillment complete,
I turn my head up to the sky
And Irresistibly laugh
At **the absurdity of destination**

The Forbidden Exit

The forbidden exit

In the depth of my abyss,
Where silence has prevailed long..
I have been excavating the self
Without the premise of time .
In the solitude of my sanctity,
In the holiness of meditation,
I have long been abandoned
Even by my own shadows.
No visitors tread this path,
No lovers cross this maze.
I have been in a communion deep
which none dare disturb.
In timeless frames,
I witnessed forms
That reminiscence of a bygone era.
Once upon a time
this world was a familiar place.
Now those lights hurt at the eye
Which is happily in accustom
To its own light...
The shun is strict,
The solitude serene..
However....if u so insist,
I will let open a crevice.
Enter ....
And bolt it back....
to exit is forbidden!

The Forbidden Return

The forbidden return

When the dates of this lifetime
have become a memory distant,
and the islands of love
that had been inhabited
with divine companions
now lies abandoned…
There will arise a new dawn
where the lean on love
stands null and void
and every pain stimulus
falls below the inciting threshold.
On this impending dawn,
at the summit of this dissolution,
Every single concept will be shunned
and the drop will be in absolute.
I will know a new freedom
to travel to enchanted lands
from which I shall **never return**

The Drop Off

The drop off

This engulfing silence
has swallowed up my words.
the absence of thought
has deprived me of all worry and fear.
this place of dispassion
where the often lived melancholy has dissolved.
Gaiety now lies abandoned
which had earlier rejoiced.
The senses are now absent
that had nourished earlier lusts.
Where every accompanied presence
has left without notice;
and there is no anticipation
of someone to halt by.
These arid zones of disenchanted stupor
have robbed me of all mistaken identities.
In this lost and misplaced era
of a frozen timelessness
I seek to know
the dynamics of this unfolding
only to discover that even the "I"
has **dropped off**

AMAVASYA... The Dark Night Of The Soul.

The Misplaced Oasis

The misplaced oasis

My parched mouth stares
at the never ending horizons of sand dunes,
my taste now, barely a memory,
as I have been plainly deprived.
The fading sun is a reminder
Of the impending death throes.
At the brink of this longing,
At the summit of this pain,
I need to summon up all gut
And strike every ounce of soil
Until **the misplaced oasis** effulges out elixir
And satiates me to bliss.

The Second Chance

The second chance

I was my best careful
As I took my last unsure steps.
I could be thrown off orbit,
Or forever denied entrance.
I had hailed an earlier few storms
And dared lightening & typhoons.
I stood ruminating,
On my previous triumphs and falls.
I was surely intelligent,
And had an impeccable memory of maps.
The risk was unparallel
And I might lose, never to return.
Thus thinking, I jumped off the cliff
Into the abyss of a screeching silence.
For a moment, I thought..I was dead.
soon; there was a grand unveiling
to a flight of golden stairs.
It was not yet time,
I had been rewarded **a second chance**

The Majestic Chaos

The majestic chaos

A lot is disintegrating..
I am largely a witness
To this fragmentation.
What will be the last one left,
I shall stay to see.
And then one fine day,
It will promptly refashion itself
Into a majestic pattern
Of profound light and awareness.
Which stars were ever born
Before the chaos that reigned in them?

The Proclamation

The proclamation

I brave the whirling winds.
Caught in the epicenter
Of the merciless blowing,
My faith like a wounded animal,
My hope tattered and torn,
A tender meek voice murmured at my ear,
"you are meant to uncover
The sacred and the strong,
The perfectness that simmers
To see the forbidden daybreak.
Just believe, breathe and let go
Of the patterns that condition, chatter and clutter you.
Resuscitate your hopes and beliefs.
Rise with a mighty roar
And proclaim the grandeur
That rightfully "You" are!

The Delusions The Semi enlightened

The delusions of the semi enlightened

Seekers suffer from maladies,
Of disillusionments, stupor and more.
The path is concealed, the trails untread.
One has to continue journeying through.
Sometimes, nirvana is an alluding farfetched dream,
At others, merely a wink away.
Gurus & guides, philosophers and friends,
Soul mates and twin flames, possessions and knowledge,
All can take us a few counted steps,
Everything seems to be a myth
And then, all is tinged by the truth.
Agonies and pangs are the hallmarks of **semi enlightenment**,
Transcending these too,
We will finally arrive.

The Way

The way

I have been lurking
Here Since late.
It has been dreary dark..
This darkness must be the way.
The way to the light
Must pass through this only.
I must travel on,
I must hold on,
To the pangs of this absence.
This alone will lead me
To the pinnacle of truth.

The Orgasm of Spring

The orgasm of spring

My wounded heart
Laced with the agonies of life,
Lurking in darkness,
Snorkeling for joy..
So lost was I,
That the note of beauty
Had been clearly misplaced.
A nature walk
Gave my eyes a clarity indeed...
The breeze had a special scent,
The aphrodisiac incense of the divine.
The leaves stood glistening green
To the peek of a distorted ray.
The flowers were here,
The fruit was near...
Reminders of the possibilities of life.
" Isn't this another lifetime?
I chose to wonder.
My melancholies had broken away
From its promises of sorrow
And stood climaxing to love...
The foreplay of winter
Had lead to **the orgasm of spring**

The Aching Solitude

The aching solitude

Happy are those
Who travel enthusiastically
To arrive to chosen locations...
To the unfortunate few,
Even these inspirations are snatched....
The myth of travel and the adventure of discovery
Both have lost their grip on me.
My Beloved God....at least u should have left me these frugal inspirations.
I bleed at places
which were earlier points of contact.
And the pity is that even pain has become mere observation.
Lost are the layers that held me safe,
Now I lie denuded to the truth....
Who can save me now
From the partnership of
This **aching solitude**

The Weeping Willow

The weeping willow

In the mid lap of a full blown spring
Where the burst of glory smiles unfeigned...
There came across a novel sight
A stark contrast from where it stood.
Not a single leaf adorned ,
Not a flower to boast of.
And at its summit
A mighty bird stood perched
Preparing to take flight.
At least it served unto its end...
It strikes a chord of dispassion
Of how it was no less unique.
Having shed all its attachments
And baring itself to the truth;
It had a dignity of its own.
An epitome of sorrow...
The weeping willow
Had barely managed in me
Some divine inspirations....

SHIVA& SHAKTI...The Amalgamation.

Kaala

Kaala

In the disdain to life
I had been eternally trapped.
Thought it was in vogue
To be unbothered and uncouth.
Through the peepholes,
You brought in beams of light
Which illuminated piles of ignorance.
Eons of illusions swiped away by a single wind.
Shiva is not about mere inebriation
Or a height of indifferent muse.
He is a presence that vibrates
In the heart of life
and in excellent and matchless perfection;
Responds to life fearlessly.
There is sacredness about him
That is hardly polite to the impious
And yet; so deeply drenched in compassion.
He is not hungry for devotion,
And yet... he accolades those who drown.
With this new version of Shiva,
You empower me with a vision
And the necessary surrender
To dissolve unto this
abyss called Kaala

Shiva...The Homecoming

Shiva: the homecoming.

Frenzy is his calling,
Anarchy, his style.
Defiance of all order,
He walks unabated unto me.
The doors had been left open,
And he slipped in.
The abandon that he is…
Has engulfed all my sanity.
Penetrating all sheaths of order,
He has rendered me into a majestic chaos.
I had strived all along for moksha,
He laughed and set me all free.
I instill his inebriation,
And my eyes a half open,
I recreate my own intensities.
Sthira as if a dead log,
Absent as if promised to be unfound…
He has flowered in me without permission,
Copulated me without shame.
I stand in divine denudement
And welcome him home.

The Ardhanareeshwara

The Ardhanareeshwara

Like the philanthropic Shiva
Who sheds his half
To welcome unto him
The mellowed Shakti..
You open up your spaces
For me to frolic and play.
All Duality lies shunned,
Only the amalgamation remains
Of Purusha and Prakriti,
Love and light,
Yin and yang.
I was once upon feminine
and then with your ejaculated pearl
I come to be known
as
The ardhanareeshwara

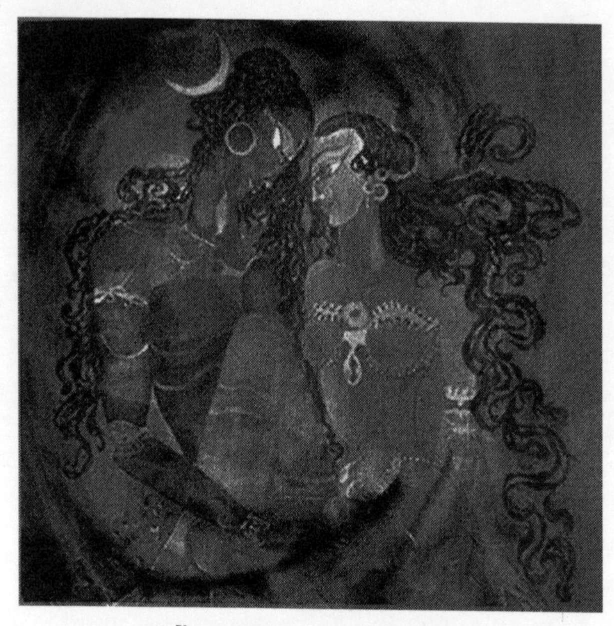

The Sambhog

The sambhog

There is not a taste of gentleness
Or the feminine flamboyance
Of a culted form..
She is a metaphor of Shakti
That empowers its own divinity.
Riding high on her vein is
Only a deep drunkenness
And longing to quench
From the depths of her secret oasis
Where Shiva is in dynamic meditation
and brinking at life giving explosion.
She will succumb to his dust
and then seduce him to her.
She knows he is an OUTLAW
And will dissolve unto none...
But she is no lesser a fire,
And this **Sacred Sambhog**
Is what our world is all about...

The Birth

The birth

I found myself in a pit dark,
It was cold and lonely here...
Time had no notion in me.
Only semi formed was I.
In my bewilderment,
I felt my limbs grow.
In my half demented state,
Midway between life and death,
A sweetness dropped by on the ear.
Ah! My first contact point with life.
You sang me a melody divine.
I tried to see, Yet vision failed.
My eyes were a painful shut.
I longed to witness the form of you
And know this sweetness first hand.
À creak happened to break the silence,
And like cracks on parched land,
You split open my cataracts..
Ah! Now I could hear and see
The one who had birthed me...
In tenderness and awe,
You held me in your loving embrace,
and smiled at my novice form.
I smiled back
In silent gratitude....
To acknowledge Shakti...the Divine Mother.

Yin & Yang

Yin & yang

In the womb of creation,
We birth in divine glory.
In the arms of mother earth,
Nurtured and provided.
In supple river beds,
We sink our roots.
All creativities, teachings & moralities
Spring forth from the divine feminine.
Denial of this life source,
Is the rejection of life.
No Shiva without Shakti,
No Yang without Yin,
In this duality of complementation,
We become healed, whole and complete.

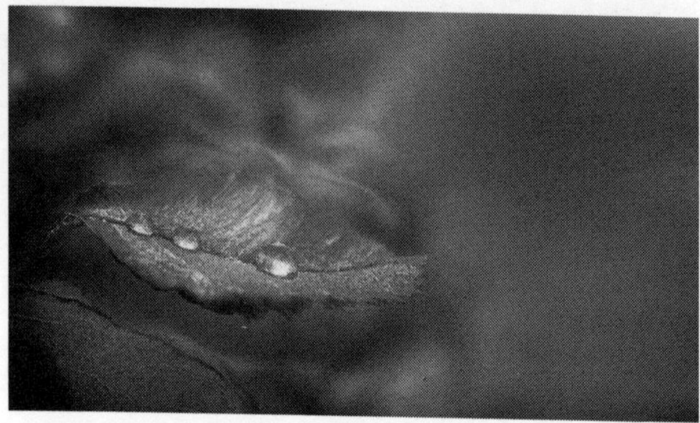

The Osmosis

The osmosis

The earth in me is parched high,
I only flame its quench
to expand unto the open skies.
from the womb of Shiva,
The rains will pour
and bring to blossom
the saplings of self realization.
I aspire not for gardens of fruits
but only to enhance
this divine **osmosis**

Shiva..The Cosmic Mind

Shiva..The Cosmic Mind

Through platonic invisible networks,
where dimensions are easily transcended,
Thoughts no longer beg for words,
Ideas relay at their mere origin,
Every appearance on the surface of consciousness
translates into an amplified signal.
Here timelessness is the ambience
and no recognition of limitation prevails.
One is multiplied to become many
and the mind merely vestigial.
Travel occurs in precision
through a faultless intelligence.
With Shiva as medium;
a wanderer has been transmuted
into the **cosmic mind.**

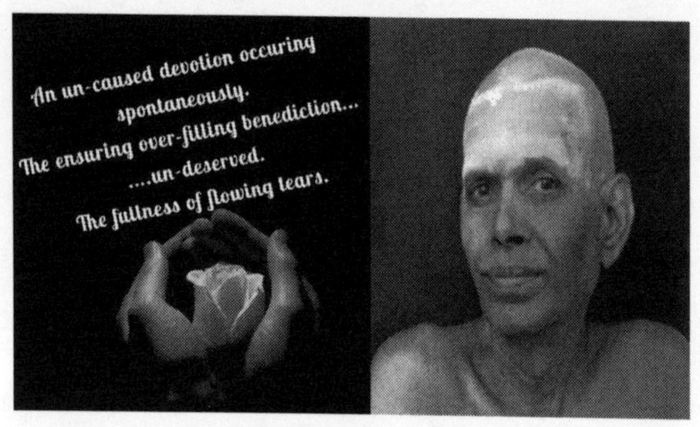

Ramana Maharishi... The Beckoning

Ramana Maharishi: The beckoning

When the magic of words is lost,
you replace them with mute exchanges.
So sweet is your fragrance,
I forgot my own.
I tread the path that leads to thee.
Will my stumbling steps find you?
you erase the paraphernalia of questions
and crash up my mental maze.
At the awaited confront,
What will I say to thou?
I travel moment to moment,
wonder at which corner you might appear.
Until then…I sing your hymns
or still to a silenced state.
My journey might be a step away
or maybe miles to go before I sleep.
Distance and time are mere illusion
when you **beckon** with such loving charm.

Ramana...The Martyr

Ramana...The martyr

Even though dead, through the buried deep,
Your fragrance still brims the winds,
The springs come to beg inspiration
And the rains to quench their age old thirst,
Many come to wail their woes
And go back embedded to peace.
This stilled detonation that lurks around you
Will explode all those who seek.
Your body has ashed to earth,
Your breath no longer flows.
Then what is this compelling tug
That encroaches and dissolves the silly "ego"?
What could be this immortal spirit
That fetches these people from faraway?
In ensuing days, I begin to know
From conversing voices..
You were a true **martyr** to love!"

An Ode To Maa Ganga

An Ode To Maa Ganga

the inkling murmurs of a ceaseless flow,
the perennial joy of just to "be",
an embrace that welcomes home
the pains, the prayers and ashes all the same.
A memoir of our dignified association
with elements in perfect harmony.
Sometimes in rage and rapid travel,
At others a ripple free entity.
So many faces and yet just one,
You bless, nourish and are divine fervor
for our soul vortexes to build anew.
You are an epitome of feminine
beauty, surrender and power
emanating from shiva's crown.
In the womb of your mesmerizing devotion,
I compose this ode of universal piety.

Arunachala...An Intended Pilgrimage To An Enlightened Void

Arunachala...An Intended Pilgrimage To An Enlightened Void

Life has a manner of passing by,
where seeking and striving are deep conditioning.
In the enthusiasm for results,
the beauty of the journey often missed.
spirituality… another mind game
where striving to moksha, a high end pursuit.
The shortest routes in the fastest time,
is the most favored way.
I had intended to be on a pilgrimage
with a similar chaste desire.
In a meditative moment, an awakening dawned.
In the ambience of Arunachala,
beneath the gaze of Ramana,
all I need to do
is to surrender in silence
and be open to receive.
no striving, reaching or even talking,
only 'being' is the qualified way.
so, I'll come to you and partake of your **enlightened void**

SAMPOORNA:The Divine Merger....A Global Embracing.

Conversations Between The Bridge The River

Conversations Between The Bridge The River

I flow on in joyous tones,
Carrying with me the silt of a forsaken time.
How do you keep so still?
I stand in service to aid crossovers.
If I'd move, my life would be in vain.
I have newer shades and faces every day,
Sometimes full, at others blue or grey,
I have to keep up a constant face
To win the trust of those I serve.
The moon is so very biased to me,
Casting on me its enlightened fullness,
I remain witness all along for lovers
Kissing on moonless nights.
I am the giver of life and bounty,
An embodiment of worship & homage,
I encourage platforms for this sacred act.
We could debate on this long.
Let us not be in oblique,
We are congruent like day & night,
Our alchemy is a gift to the world.

The Satori

The Satori

In the dim lit shadows,
That lurked at my windows,
I happened to presence a visitor.
It was a gloomy evening,
I had packed up for the day
And returned to my reminiscences, memoirs and more.
The previous days had scarred and bled me.
I needed to rediscover my oblivion,
And brood a little on life.
So, here I was, all set to dissolve.
Who was it at this hour,
This very unwanted visitor?
I sighed a heavy breath
And moved reluctantly to the door.
I had a second thought
Of rejecting this advance.
With a dilemma still playing in me,
I creaked the door open.
I was greeted by a light
That shone straight at my heart.
A peaceful stillness descended on my raging mind,

A love water falled at my heart's abode.
All desires put together
Had not satiated me such.
Everything was now completely complete.
I rushed outside to boast of this glory,
Alas....I had lost my voice!

The edge...where substance
and shadow...meet...merge and
consume each other.

The Same

The Same

In the often not spoken words,
In the answers to mundane queries,
In the longings that knock at the heart,
In the arms that open to embrace,
In the eyes that shed tears,
In the sharing when it's not enough,
In the knowing and yet forgiving,
In the sleep and yet, being aware,
In the loneliness and offering intimacy,
In the grieving and yet supporting,
One knows ,for sure
That each of us are **the same**

The Qualia

The Qualia

The world and its noise
slowly recedes and submerges in the backdrop,
Many pages left undone,
Many a word left unsaid,
The frenzy of lighted celebrations
drops dead in the quagmire of darkness.
The strings of pleasure, pain & desire
snap off in this zone of absence.
All worldly relations drop dead at this door,
which every man ought enter alone.
The body merely a cloak heavy,
that one would be delighted to shed,
The mind numbed in infancy
to its most juvenile state.
All aspiration, ambition and striving
a senseless load of the ailing mind!
When the eyelashes shed all inhibition
and droop, to shut out the glossy world.
In the sanctity of meditation,
come alive the newest perceptions.
The denseness in me is cloud light.
no adornments on my naked truth.

Dimensions and portals beyond the physical,
I fly in freedom to the astral worlds.
in the treasure house of meditation,
lie the diamonds and rubies
of my sacred **qualias**

The Skyfallen

The Skyfallen

Through the dense darkness
The overhanging submerged void,
There come along flashes of light.
One could easily mistake them
For a shattered star scatter.
And pass them off as naught.
At the impinge of the heralding dawn,
When the melodies of silence sing at their peak,
These flashes come with an amplified clarity.
And now I witness them as majestic stars,
They have graced me from mystic lands.
And they are truly
skyfallen

The Universal Devotee

The Universal Devotee

I started out as agnostic,
Then on love befell.
How had I survived these years,
I wondered in deep applause?
My days were brighter, my songs were joy,
And then one ordinary day,
Love taught me the final finest lesson,
Of how to let go..
The ache was silent, I bled at nights.
At the dawn of this dark night of the soul,
I was shown zones of light
Here, I was still very loved.
So, like a child, I held it in clasp
Until it soon became core.
And every beauty made me wail,
Boundaries of self and the other
Losing out in merging forms
Until all fused into a divine formlessness
With me sinking into a global compassion.
Karuna in my hridyam,
Devotion in my veins,
I was transmuted
From a lover
To **The universal devotee.**

The Spiritual Dignity

The Spiritual Dignity

When the misplaced gods in us have finally awakened,
When the "I" is a projection of the global icon,
When mighty compassion has replaced petty love,
When a single tear salts a million mouths,
When kindness is the crown of strength,
and wisdom the way of life,
When beauty is the highlighted asset,
and gratitude the highest honour,
When freedom is the valuable glory,
and laughter the grandest adorn,
When joy is a must over spill,
When the universe is a unilateral consciousness,
and no borders tear our hearts apart,
We will rejoice
in the lap
of
our **spiritual dignity.**

The Dignified Association

The Dignified Association

What worth is a lute
Without the lips that laze at its form?
What worth is the sky,
Without the stars that adorn its bosom?
What worth is a blooming rose,
If butterflies don't flock to its form?
What worth is my beloved God,
If I pour not on him my love?
The dignity of association
Is what keeps the binary alive.

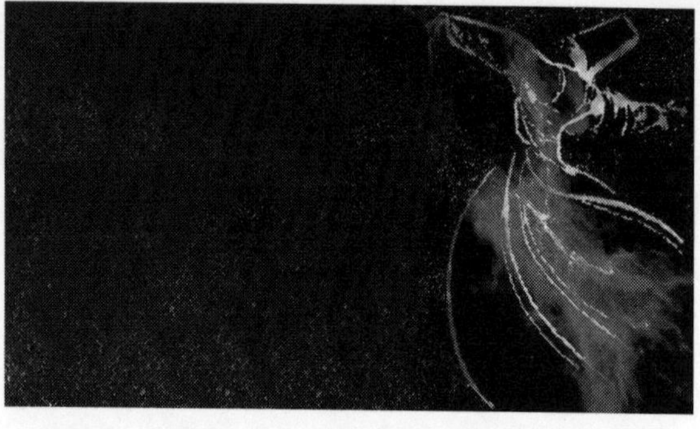

The Dervish

The Dervish

Who else other than you
Is the lead in all my stories?
I have sculpted my heart
To be able and enough vessel.
When you pour,
I'll drink with my lips attuned
And then on the beholden night,
When the antique moon
Bursts at my horizon
I'll come to swirl and swirl
Until the bug of delight
Has consumed me full;
When both the swirling
And **the dervish** in me
Have been dissolved
Unto your almighty presence.

The Throne Of Infinity

The Throne Of Infinity

I Have denied my divinity long
Slithering in the burrows of karma.
Tatters of the mind hang loosely
On the yoke of a misidentified body.
There are emotions that spur
And arise sluggishly from the being
Sometimes eroding awareness
And mistaking one to be them.
At this awaited dawn,
I have been rendered
Open at both ends.
Where the melody
Spills from a full brim
Like a reed that has been graced
With the Midas lips at it.
Now ..I sit bequeathed
Crowned with the platinum rewards
And rule like God
From my **throne of infinity**

The Myth Of Adam & Eve

The Myth Of Adam & Eve

The highlighted adultery
That defamed them far....
The fall from sanctity,
The Loss of a sacred virginity....
Who can toss for this forbidden act?
What really brought about it all?
Awareness was the defaulter.
Watching their nakedness,
The veil of lust befell their senses...
They had lived in an abandon divine,
Now sought each other as wine.
The sight had intoxicated,
the demeanor let loose..
The flip side of a sacredness,
That the world had known unto then.
But can they be truly blamed
For God's intended act?
They merely played their roles.
Then why be driven to blame?
It's time we let go of
The myth of Adam and Eve.